50 Mexican Dessert and Sweet Recipes for Home

By: Kelly Johnson

Table of Contents

- Tres Leches Cake
- Churros with Chocolate Sauce
- Flan (Caramel Custard)
- Arroz con Leche (Rice Pudding)
- Mexican Wedding Cookies (Polvorones)
- Pastel de Elote (Corn Cake)
- Sopapillas
- Champurrado (Mexican Hot Chocolate)
- Bunuelos
- Cajeta (Dulce de Leche)
- Capirotada (Mexican Bread Pudding)
- Conchas (Mexican Sweet Bread)
- Mangonadas (Mango Sorbet)
- Mexican Chocolate Torte
- Rosca de Reyes (King's Cake)
- Cocadas (Coconut Candies)
- Pineapple Empanadas
- Alfajores (Dulce de Leche Sandwich Cookies)
- Mexican Fruit Salad with Chili Powder
- Atole (Mexican Hot Cornmeal Drink)
- Mazapan (Mexican Peanut Candy)
- Cinnamon Sugar Buñuelos
- Caramel Flan
- Arroz con Leche (Mexican Rice Pudding)
- Bionico (Mexican Fruit Salad)
- Cinnamon Churro Cheesecake Bars
- Mexican Chocolate Ice Cream
- Mexican Wedding Cake (Pastel de Tres Leches)
- Coconut Tres Leches Cake
- Mexican Hot Chocolate Brownies
- Cinnamon Sugar Sopapilla Cheesecake Bars
- Mexican Chocolate Tiramisu
- Horchata (Mexican Rice Drink)
- Tamarind Candy (Mexican Dulce de Tamarindo)
- Coconut Flan

- Cajeta Crepes
- Chocolate Tamale
- Pineapple Upside Down Cake with a Twist
- Mexican Mango Ice Cream (Nieve de Mango)
- Sopaipilla Cheesecake Bars
- Mexican Chocolate Mousse
- Buñuelos de Viento (Mexican Wind Fritters)
- Mexican Coconut Lime Bars
- Chocolate Abuelita Cupcakes
- Mexican Brownies with Pecans
- Mexican Orange Cake
- Lime Margarita Bars
- Chocolate Avocado Mousse
- Pumpkin Empanadas
- Mexican Chocolate Chip Cookies

Tres Leches Cake

Ingredients:

For the Cake:

- 1 cup all-purpose flour
- 1 1/2 teaspoons baking powder
- 1/4 teaspoon salt
- 5 large eggs, separated
- 1 cup granulated sugar, divided
- 1/3 cup whole milk
- 1 teaspoon vanilla extract

For the Milk Mixture:

- 1 can (14 ounces) sweetened condensed milk
- 1 can (12 ounces) evaporated milk
- 1 cup whole milk

For the Topping:

- 2 cups heavy cream
- 2 tablespoons powdered sugar
- 1 teaspoon vanilla extract

Instructions:

Preheat your oven to 350°F (175°C). Grease and flour a 9x13-inch baking dish.
In a medium bowl, sift together the flour, baking powder, and salt. Set aside.
In a large mixing bowl, beat the egg whites on high speed until soft peaks form. Gradually add in 1/2 cup of granulated sugar, continuing to beat until stiff peaks form. Set aside.
In another large mixing bowl, beat the egg yolks with the remaining 1/2 cup of granulated sugar until pale and fluffy. Mix in the milk and vanilla extract.
Gently fold the flour mixture into the egg yolk mixture until just combined.
Carefully fold in the beaten egg whites until no streaks remain.

Pour the batter into the prepared baking dish and spread it out evenly.

Bake in the preheated oven for 25 to 30 minutes, or until a toothpick inserted into the center comes out clean.

While the cake is baking, prepare the milk mixture by combining the sweetened condensed milk, evaporated milk, and whole milk in a bowl. Mix well.

Once the cake is done baking and while it's still hot, use a fork or skewer to poke holes all over the top of the cake.

Slowly pour the milk mixture over the hot cake, allowing it to soak in. Let the cake cool completely in the refrigerator for at least 1 hour, preferably longer or overnight.

Before serving, whip the heavy cream with powdered sugar and vanilla extract until stiff peaks form. Spread the whipped cream over the top of the chilled cake.

Serve cold and enjoy the creamy goodness of Tres Leches Cake!

This cake is incredibly moist and rich, with the perfect balance of sweetness from the milk mixture and the lightness of the whipped cream topping. It's sure to be a hit at any gathering or celebration!

Churros with Chocolate Sauce

Ingredients:

For the Churros:

- 1 cup water
- 2 1/2 tablespoons granulated sugar
- 1/2 teaspoon salt
- 2 tablespoons vegetable oil
- 1 cup all-purpose flour
- Vegetable oil, for frying

For Coating:

- 1/4 cup granulated sugar
- 1 teaspoon ground cinnamon

For the Chocolate Sauce:

- 1/2 cup heavy cream
- 1 cup semi-sweet chocolate chips
- 1/2 teaspoon vanilla extract

Instructions:

In a saucepan, combine water, sugar, salt, and vegetable oil. Bring to a boil over medium-high heat.
Remove the saucepan from the heat and add the flour all at once. Stir vigorously until the mixture forms a ball and pulls away from the sides of the pan.
Heat vegetable oil in a deep skillet or frying pan over medium-high heat until it reaches 350°F (175°C).
Spoon the churro dough into a piping bag fitted with a large star tip.
Carefully pipe strips of dough into the hot oil, using kitchen scissors to cut them to your desired length. Fry the churros until golden brown and crisp, about 2-3 minutes per side.
Remove the cooked churros from the oil using a slotted spoon and drain them on paper towels briefly.
In a shallow dish, mix together the granulated sugar and ground cinnamon for coating. Roll the warm churros in the cinnamon sugar mixture until coated evenly.

For the chocolate sauce, heat the heavy cream in a small saucepan over medium heat until it just starts to simmer. Remove from heat and stir in the chocolate chips and vanilla extract until smooth and creamy.
Serve the warm churros immediately with the chocolate sauce for dipping.

Enjoy the crispy exterior and soft, fluffy interior of the churros dipped into the rich and indulgent chocolate sauce. It's a delightful treat that's perfect for any occasion!

Flan (Caramel Custard)

Ingredients:

For the Caramel:

- 1 cup granulated sugar
- 1/4 cup water

For the Custard:

- 4 large eggs
- 2 cups whole milk
- 1 teaspoon vanilla extract
- 1 can (14 ounces) sweetened condensed milk
- Pinch of salt

Instructions:

Preheat your oven to 350°F (175°C).
In a small saucepan, combine the granulated sugar and water for the caramel. Cook over medium heat, stirring occasionally, until the sugar dissolves.
Once the sugar has dissolved, stop stirring and let the mixture boil. Continue to cook, swirling the pan occasionally, until the mixture turns a deep amber color, about 6-8 minutes. Be careful not to burn it.
Quickly pour the caramel into a round baking dish, tilting the dish to coat the bottom evenly. Work fast as the caramel will harden quickly. Set aside to cool and harden.
In a mixing bowl, beat the eggs until well blended. Add the whole milk, sweetened condensed milk, vanilla extract, and a pinch of salt. Mix until smooth and well combined.
Pour the custard mixture over the cooled caramel in the baking dish.
Place the baking dish in a larger roasting pan or baking dish. Fill the larger dish with enough hot water to reach halfway up the sides of the baking dish with the custard mixture. This water bath (bain-marie) will help the flan cook evenly.

Carefully transfer the setup to the preheated oven and bake for about 50-60 minutes, or until the flan is set around the edges but still slightly jiggly in the center.

Once done, remove the flan from the oven and from the water bath. Let it cool to room temperature, then refrigerate for at least 4 hours or preferably overnight to chill and set completely.

To serve, run a knife around the edges of the flan to loosen it. Place a serving plate upside down over the baking dish and quickly invert to release the flan onto the plate, allowing the caramel to flow over the top.

Slice and serve the flan chilled, with the caramel sauce drizzled over each portion.

Enjoy the creamy and silky texture of this classic Flan with its rich caramel flavor. It's a delightful dessert that's sure to impress!

Arroz con Leche (Rice Pudding)

Ingredients:

- 1 cup long-grain white rice
- 4 cups whole milk
- 1 cinnamon stick
- 1/2 cup granulated sugar
- 1 teaspoon vanilla extract
- Pinch of salt
- Ground cinnamon, for garnish (optional)
- Raisins, for garnish (optional)

Instructions:

Rinse the rice under cold water until the water runs clear. This helps remove excess starch.
In a large saucepan, combine the rinsed rice, milk, and cinnamon stick. Bring to a simmer over medium heat, stirring occasionally to prevent the rice from sticking to the bottom of the pan.
Once the mixture comes to a simmer, reduce the heat to low and let it simmer gently, stirring occasionally, for about 25-30 minutes or until the rice is tender and the mixture has thickened to a creamy consistency.
Stir in the granulated sugar, vanilla extract, and a pinch of salt. Continue to cook for an additional 5-10 minutes, stirring occasionally, until the sugar has dissolved and the flavors are well combined.
Remove the saucepan from the heat and discard the cinnamon stick.
Transfer the Arroz con Leche to a serving bowl or individual serving cups. Let it cool slightly before serving.
If desired, sprinkle ground cinnamon over the top for garnish and add raisins for extra flavor.
Serve the Arroz con Leche warm or chilled, depending on your preference.

This creamy and comforting rice pudding is perfect for any occasion, whether it's a cozy family dinner or a festive celebration. Enjoy the comforting flavors of cinnamon, vanilla, and creamy rice in every spoonful!

Mexican Wedding Cookies (Polvorones)

Ingredients:

- 1 cup unsalted butter, softened
- 1/2 cup powdered sugar, plus extra for coating
- 1 teaspoon vanilla extract
- 2 cups all-purpose flour
- 1 cup finely chopped pecans or walnuts

Instructions:

Preheat your oven to 350°F (175°C). Line a baking sheet with parchment paper or silicone baking mat.
In a large mixing bowl, cream together the softened butter and powdered sugar until light and fluffy.
Mix in the vanilla extract until well combined.
Gradually add the flour to the butter mixture, mixing until a smooth dough forms.
Stir in the finely chopped nuts until evenly distributed throughout the dough.
Shape the dough into 1-inch balls and place them on the prepared baking sheet, spacing them about 1 inch apart.
Bake in the preheated oven for 12-15 minutes, or until the cookies are set but not browned.
Remove the cookies from the oven and let them cool on the baking sheet for a few minutes.
While the cookies are still warm, roll them in powdered sugar until completely coated. Place the coated cookies on a wire rack to cool completely.
Once the cookies have cooled, roll them in powdered sugar again for a second coating, if desired.
Store the Mexican Wedding Cookies in an airtight container at room temperature for up to a week.

These melt-in-your-mouth cookies are buttery, nutty, and perfectly sweet with a delicate crumb. They are a delightful treat for weddings, holidays, or any occasion where you want to indulge in a little taste of Mexico! Enjoy!

Pastel de Elote (Corn Cake)

Ingredients:

- 4 cups fresh corn kernels (about 4-5 ears of corn) or frozen corn, thawed
- 1/2 cup granulated sugar
- 1/4 cup unsalted butter, melted
- 4 large eggs
- 1/2 cup whole milk
- 1/4 cup cornmeal
- 1 teaspoon baking powder
- 1/2 teaspoon salt
- 1 teaspoon vanilla extract
- Zest of 1 lime (optional)

Instructions:

Preheat your oven to 350°F (175°C). Grease a 9-inch round cake pan or pie dish. In a blender or food processor, pulse the corn kernels until they are slightly broken down but still chunky. You don't want a completely smooth puree; some texture is desirable.

In a large mixing bowl, combine the pulsed corn kernels, granulated sugar, melted butter, eggs, milk, cornmeal, baking powder, salt, vanilla extract, and lime zest (if using). Mix until well combined.

Pour the corn cake batter into the prepared cake pan, spreading it out evenly. Bake in the preheated oven for 45-50 minutes, or until the cake is set and golden brown on top. A toothpick inserted into the center should come out clean.

Remove the cake from the oven and let it cool in the pan for about 10 minutes. After cooling slightly, run a knife around the edges of the cake to loosen it from the pan. Carefully invert the cake onto a serving platter or plate.

Serve the Pastel de Elote warm or at room temperature, optionally garnished with a sprinkle of powdered sugar, a dollop of whipped cream, or a drizzle of caramel sauce.

This moist and flavorful corn cake is a wonderful dessert or snack that celebrates the natural sweetness of fresh corn. It's perfect for enjoying alongside a cup of coffee or as a sweet treat any time of day!

Sopapillas

Ingredients:

- 2 cups all-purpose flour
- 1 teaspoon baking powder
- 1/2 teaspoon salt
- 2 tablespoons granulated sugar
- 2 tablespoons vegetable oil
- 2/3 cup warm water
- Vegetable oil, for frying
- Honey or powdered sugar, for serving (optional)

Instructions:

In a large mixing bowl, combine the flour, baking powder, salt, and granulated sugar.
Add the vegetable oil to the dry ingredients and mix until the mixture resembles coarse crumbs.
Gradually add the warm water, mixing until a soft dough forms. You may need to adjust the amount of water slightly to achieve the right consistency.
Turn the dough out onto a lightly floured surface and knead it gently for a few minutes until smooth. Cover the dough with a clean kitchen towel and let it rest for about 15-20 minutes.
After the dough has rested, divide it into smaller portions and roll each portion out into a thin circle, about 1/8 to 1/4 inch thick.
Heat vegetable oil in a deep skillet or frying pan over medium-high heat until it reaches about 350°F (175°C).
Carefully place a piece of rolled-out dough into the hot oil, frying it until it puffs up and turns golden brown on one side, about 30 seconds to 1 minute. Then, flip it over and fry the other side until golden brown.
Once cooked, remove the sopapilla from the oil using a slotted spoon or tongs and drain it on paper towels to remove excess oil.
Repeat the frying process with the remaining pieces of dough, being careful not to overcrowd the pan.
Serve the warm sopapillas immediately, drizzled with honey or sprinkled with powdered sugar, if desired.

These light and fluffy fried dough pillows are best enjoyed fresh and warm, with their crispy exterior and soft, pillowy interior. They make a delightful dessert or snack that's sure to be a hit with family and friends!

Champurrado (Mexican Hot Chocolate)

Ingredients:

- 4 cups water
- 2 cups whole milk
- 3/4 cup masa harina (corn flour)
- 1 tablet (about 3 ounces) Mexican chocolate, such as Abuelita or Ibarra, chopped
- 1/2 cup granulated sugar, or to taste
- 1 cinnamon stick
- 1 teaspoon vanilla extract
- Pinch of salt

Instructions:

In a large saucepan, combine the water and milk. Heat over medium heat until it begins to simmer, then reduce the heat to low to keep it warm.

In a separate bowl, whisk together the masa harina with a little bit of water to make a smooth paste, ensuring there are no lumps.

Gradually whisk the masa harina paste into the warm water and milk mixture until well combined. Stir constantly to prevent any lumps from forming.

Add the chopped Mexican chocolate, granulated sugar, cinnamon stick, vanilla extract, and a pinch of salt to the saucepan. Stir well to combine.

Continue to cook the Champurrado over low heat, stirring frequently, until the chocolate is completely melted and the mixture has thickened to your desired consistency. This typically takes about 15-20 minutes.

Once the Champurrado has reached the desired thickness, remove the cinnamon stick and discard it.

Taste the Champurrado and adjust the sweetness as needed by adding more sugar, if desired.

Serve the Champurrado hot in mugs or cups.

Optionally, garnish each serving with a sprinkle of ground cinnamon or a dollop of whipped cream.

Champurrado is a comforting and indulgent drink, perfect for warming up on cold days or for enjoying as a sweet treat any time of year. Its rich chocolate flavor combined with the subtle hint of cinnamon makes it a beloved favorite in Mexican cuisine. Enjoy!

Bunuelos

Ingredients:

For the Dough:

- 2 cups all-purpose flour
- 1 teaspoon baking powder
- 1/4 teaspoon salt
- 2 tablespoons granulated sugar
- 2 tablespoons unsalted butter, melted
- 2/3 cup warm water

For Frying:

- Vegetable oil, for frying

For Coating:

- 1/2 cup granulated sugar
- 1 teaspoon ground cinnamon

Instructions:

In a large mixing bowl, combine the flour, baking powder, salt, and granulated sugar.
Add the melted butter to the dry ingredients and mix until well combined.
Gradually add the warm water to the flour mixture, mixing until a smooth dough forms. You may need to adjust the amount of water slightly to achieve the right consistency. The dough should be soft and pliable, but not too sticky.
Turn the dough out onto a lightly floured surface and knead it for a few minutes until smooth. Cover the dough with a clean kitchen towel and let it rest for about 30 minutes.
After the dough has rested, divide it into smaller portions and roll each portion out into a thin circle, about 1/8 inch thick.
Heat vegetable oil in a deep skillet or frying pan over medium-high heat until it reaches about 350°F (175°C).
Carefully place a piece of rolled-out dough into the hot oil, frying it until it puffs up and turns golden brown on one side, about 1-2 minutes. Then, flip it over and fry the other side until golden brown.

Once cooked, remove the buñuelo from the oil using a slotted spoon or tongs and drain it on paper towels to remove excess oil.

Repeat the frying process with the remaining pieces of dough, being careful not to overcrowd the pan.

In a shallow dish, mix together the granulated sugar and ground cinnamon for coating.

While the buñuelos are still warm, roll them in the cinnamon sugar mixture until completely coated.

Serve the buñuelos warm or at room temperature.

Buñuelos are best enjoyed fresh and warm, with their crispy exterior and sweet cinnamon sugar coating. They make a delightful dessert or snack that's sure to be a hit with family and friends!

Cajeta (Dulce de Leche)

Ingredients:

- 4 cups goat's milk (you can also use cow's milk)
- 1 cup granulated sugar
- 1/2 teaspoon baking soda
- 1 cinnamon stick (optional)
- 1 teaspoon vanilla extract (optional)

Instructions:

In a large, heavy-bottomed saucepan, combine the goat's milk, granulated sugar, and baking soda. Stir well to combine.

Place the saucepan over medium heat and bring the mixture to a gentle boil, stirring frequently to prevent scorching.

Once the mixture comes to a boil, reduce the heat to low and let it simmer uncovered. Stir occasionally to prevent sticking and ensure even cooking.

If using a cinnamon stick, add it to the saucepan to infuse flavor. You can also add vanilla extract at this point for additional flavor, if desired.

Let the mixture simmer on low heat for about 1.5 to 2 hours, or until it thickens to a caramel-like consistency. Stir occasionally during this time.

As the mixture cooks, it will gradually darken in color and thicken. Be patient and continue cooking until it reaches your desired thickness.

Once the Cajeta has thickened to your liking, remove the cinnamon stick if used, and let the sauce cool slightly.

Transfer the Cajeta to sterilized jars or containers. It will continue to thicken as it cools.

Allow the Cajeta to cool completely before sealing the jars and storing them in the refrigerator. It will keep for several weeks when stored properly.

Serve the Cajeta drizzled over ice cream, pancakes, waffles, or use it as a dip for fruit. You can also spread it on toast or use it as a filling for pastries and cakes.

Homemade Cajeta is rich, creamy, and full of caramel flavor, making it a delightful addition to many desserts and snacks. Enjoy this traditional Mexican treat!

Capirotada (Mexican Bread Pudding)

Ingredients:

- 8 cups stale bolillo or French bread, cut into 1-inch cubes
- 2 cups grated cheese (traditionally, Mexican queso fresco or Monterey Jack cheese is used)
- 1 cup raisins
- 1 cup chopped pecans or walnuts
- 1 cup dried apricots, chopped
- 1 cup dried prunes, chopped
- 1 cinnamon stick
- 1 whole clove
- 2 cups water
- 1 cone of piloncillo (about 8 ounces), or 1 cup packed brown sugar
- 1 tablespoon ground cinnamon
- 1/4 teaspoon ground cloves
- Butter or cooking spray, for greasing the baking dish

Instructions:

Preheat your oven to 350°F (175°C). Grease a 9x13-inch baking dish with butter or cooking spray.

In a medium saucepan, combine the water, piloncillo or brown sugar, cinnamon stick, and whole clove. Bring to a simmer over medium heat, stirring occasionally, until the piloncillo or sugar is completely dissolved. Remove from heat and set aside.

In a large mixing bowl, combine the bread cubes, grated cheese, raisins, chopped nuts, dried apricots, and dried prunes. Toss to mix evenly.

Transfer half of the bread mixture to the prepared baking dish and spread it out evenly.

Drizzle half of the piloncillo syrup over the bread mixture in the baking dish.

Add the remaining bread mixture on top, followed by the remaining piloncillo syrup.

Sprinkle ground cinnamon and ground cloves evenly over the top.

Cover the baking dish with aluminum foil and bake in the preheated oven for 30 minutes.

After 30 minutes, remove the foil and bake for an additional 15-20 minutes, or until the top is golden brown and the bread pudding is set.

Remove the baking dish from the oven and let the Capirotada cool for a few minutes before serving.

Serve the Capirotada warm, scooping out portions with a spoon. Enjoy the delicious blend of sweet and savory flavors!

Capirotada is often served during Lent and other special occasions in Mexican households. It's a comforting and satisfying dessert that's perfect for sharing with family and friends. Enjoy!

Conchas (Mexican Sweet Bread)

Ingredients:

- 8 cups stale bolillo or French bread, cut into 1-inch cubes
- 2 cups grated cheese (traditionally, Mexican queso fresco or Monterey Jack cheese is used)
- 1 cup raisins
- 1 cup chopped pecans or walnuts
- 1 cup dried apricots, chopped
- 1 cup dried prunes, chopped
- 1 cinnamon stick
- 1 whole clove
- 2 cups water
- 1 cone of piloncillo (about 8 ounces), or 1 cup packed brown sugar
- 1 tablespoon ground cinnamon
- 1/4 teaspoon ground cloves
- Butter or cooking spray, for greasing the baking dish

Instructions:

Preheat your oven to 350°F (175°C). Grease a 9x13-inch baking dish with butter or cooking spray.

In a medium saucepan, combine the water, piloncillo or brown sugar, cinnamon stick, and whole clove. Bring to a simmer over medium heat, stirring occasionally, until the piloncillo or sugar is completely dissolved. Remove from heat and set aside.

In a large mixing bowl, combine the bread cubes, grated cheese, raisins, chopped nuts, dried apricots, and dried prunes. Toss to mix evenly.

Transfer half of the bread mixture to the prepared baking dish and spread it out evenly.

Drizzle half of the piloncillo syrup over the bread mixture in the baking dish.

Add the remaining bread mixture on top, followed by the remaining piloncillo syrup.

Sprinkle ground cinnamon and ground cloves evenly over the top.

Cover the baking dish with aluminum foil and bake in the preheated oven for 30 minutes.

After 30 minutes, remove the foil and bake for an additional 15-20 minutes, or until the top is golden brown and the bread pudding is set.

Remove the baking dish from the oven and let the Capirotada cool for a few minutes before serving.

Serve the Capirotada warm, scooping out portions with a spoon. Enjoy the delicious blend of sweet and savory flavors!

Capirotada is often served during Lent and other special occasions in Mexican households. It's a comforting and satisfying dessert that's perfect for sharing with family and friends. Enjoy!

Mangonadas (Mango Sorbet)

Ingredients:

- 4 ripe mangoes, peeled and diced (fresh or frozen)
- 1/4 cup chamoy sauce (available at Mexican grocery stores or online)
- 1/4 cup lime juice
- 2 tablespoons granulated sugar (optional, adjust to taste)
- 1/2 teaspoon chili powder (Tajin or similar)
- Tajin or chili powder, for rimming glasses (optional)
- Fresh mango slices, for garnish (optional)
- Tajin-covered straws or spoons, for serving (optional)

Instructions:

Place the diced mangoes in a blender or food processor.
Add the chamoy sauce, lime juice, granulated sugar (if using), and chili powder to the blender.
Blend the mixture until smooth and creamy. Taste and adjust the sweetness and spiciness by adding more sugar or chili powder if desired.
If you prefer a smoother texture, you can strain the mango mixture through a fine-mesh sieve to remove any fibrous bits.
Pour the mango mixture into popsicle molds or an ice cream maker, following the manufacturer's instructions to freeze or churn until it reaches a sorbet-like consistency.
If you don't have popsicle molds or an ice cream maker, you can pour the mango mixture into a shallow dish and freeze it, stirring occasionally to break up any ice crystals until it firms up.
While the mango sorbet is freezing, you can prepare the glasses by rimming them with Tajin or chili powder for an extra kick of flavor.
Once the mango sorbet is ready, scoop it into serving glasses or bowls.
Garnish each serving with fresh mango slices if desired, and serve immediately with Tajin-covered straws or spoons for an added flavor boost.
Enjoy your homemade Mangonadas as a refreshing and flavorful treat on a hot day!

Mangonadas are a delightful combination of sweet, tangy, and spicy flavors that are sure to cool you down and satisfy your taste buds. Experiment with the ingredients and adjust the sweetness and spiciness to suit your preferences. Enjoy!

Mexican Chocolate Torte

Ingredients:

For the Torte:

- 1 cup unsalted butter
- 8 ounces bittersweet chocolate, chopped
- 1 cup granulated sugar
- 1/2 cup packed brown sugar
- 4 large eggs
- 1 teaspoon vanilla extract
- 1 cup all-purpose flour
- 1/4 cup cocoa powder
- 1 teaspoon ground cinnamon
- 1/2 teaspoon chili powder (optional)
- 1/2 teaspoon salt

For the Chocolate Ganache:

- 1 cup heavy cream
- 8 ounces bittersweet chocolate, chopped

For Garnish (optional):

- Whipped cream
- Berries
- Cocoa powder for dusting
- Chili powder for garnish

Instructions:

Preheat your oven to 350°F (175°C). Grease a 9-inch round cake pan and line the bottom with parchment paper.
In a medium saucepan, melt the butter and chopped bittersweet chocolate over low heat, stirring frequently, until smooth. Remove from heat and let it cool slightly.

In a large mixing bowl, whisk together the granulated sugar, brown sugar, eggs, and vanilla extract until well combined.

Gradually add the melted chocolate mixture to the egg mixture, whisking constantly until smooth.

In a separate bowl, sift together the flour, cocoa powder, ground cinnamon, chili powder (if using), and salt.

Gradually add the dry ingredients to the wet ingredients, folding gently until just combined. Do not overmix.

Pour the batter into the prepared cake pan and spread it out evenly.

Bake in the preheated oven for 30-35 minutes, or until a toothpick inserted into the center comes out with moist crumbs clinging to it.

Remove the torte from the oven and let it cool in the pan for about 10 minutes before transferring it to a wire rack to cool completely.

While the torte is cooling, prepare the chocolate ganache. In a small saucepan, heat the heavy cream over medium heat until it just starts to simmer.

Remove from heat and add the chopped bittersweet chocolate to the saucepan. Let it sit for a minute, then stir until smooth and glossy.

Let the ganache cool slightly until it thickens to a spreadable consistency.

Once the torte has cooled completely, spread the chocolate ganache over the top and sides of the torte.

If desired, garnish the torte with whipped cream, berries, a dusting of cocoa powder, and a sprinkle of chili powder for an extra kick.

Slice and serve the Mexican Chocolate Torte, and enjoy the rich and indulgent flavors!

This Mexican Chocolate Torte is sure to impress with its rich chocolate flavor enhanced by hints of cinnamon and chili, all topped off with a luscious chocolate ganache. It's the perfect dessert for any special occasion or celebration!

Rosca de Reyes (King's Cake)

Ingredients:

For the Dough:

- 4 cups all-purpose flour
- 1/2 cup granulated sugar
- 1 teaspoon salt
- 1 tablespoon active dry yeast
- 3/4 cup warm milk
- 1/2 cup unsalted butter, melted
- 3 large eggs
- 1 teaspoon vanilla extract
- Zest of 1 orange
- Zest of 1 lemon

For the Decoration:

- 1 egg, beaten (for egg wash)
- Candied fruit (such as cherries, figs, or citrus peel)
- Sliced almonds (optional)
- Sugar crystals or pearl sugar (optional)

For the Glaze:

- 1 cup powdered sugar
- 2-3 tablespoons milk
- 1/2 teaspoon vanilla extract

Instructions:

In a small bowl, dissolve the yeast in warm milk with a pinch of sugar. Let it sit for about 5-10 minutes, until frothy.
In a large mixing bowl, combine the flour, sugar, and salt. Make a well in the center and add the yeast mixture, melted butter, eggs, vanilla extract, orange zest, and lemon zest.

Mix the ingredients until a dough forms. Knead the dough on a floured surface for about 8-10 minutes, until smooth and elastic.

Place the dough in a greased bowl, cover with a clean kitchen towel, and let it rise in a warm place for about 1-2 hours, or until doubled in size.

Once the dough has risen, punch it down and divide it into two equal portions. Roll each portion into a long rope and twist them together to form a ring. Pinch the ends together to seal and transfer the ring to a greased baking sheet.

Cover the dough with a clean kitchen towel and let it rise for another 30-45 minutes, until puffed up.

Preheat your oven to 350°F (175°C). Brush the risen dough with beaten egg for a shiny finish.

Decorate the top of the Rosca with candied fruit, sliced almonds, and sugar crystals or pearl sugar, if desired.

Bake in the preheated oven for 25-30 minutes, or until the Rosca is golden brown and sounds hollow when tapped on the bottom.

While the Rosca is baking, prepare the glaze by whisking together powdered sugar, milk, and vanilla extract until smooth.

Once the Rosca is done baking, remove it from the oven and let it cool on a wire rack.

Once cooled, drizzle the glaze over the Rosca de Reyes.

Serve the Rosca de Reyes sliced and enjoy with hot chocolate or coffee.

Rosca de Reyes is a delicious and festive dessert that is enjoyed by families and friends during the Epiphany celebration. It's often served with hot chocolate or atole and is a symbol of the Three Wise Men's visit to baby Jesus. Enjoy this special treat with your loved ones!

Cocadas (Coconut Candies)

Ingredients:

- 3 cups shredded sweetened coconut
- 1 cup granulated sugar
- 2 large egg whites
- 1/4 teaspoon vanilla extract
- Pinch of salt

Instructions:

Preheat your oven to 325°F (160°C). Line a baking sheet with parchment paper or silicone baking mat.
In a large mixing bowl, combine the shredded coconut, granulated sugar, vanilla extract, and salt. Mix well to combine.
In a separate clean mixing bowl, beat the egg whites with a whisk or electric mixer until stiff peaks form.
Gently fold the beaten egg whites into the coconut mixture until everything is evenly combined. Be careful not to deflate the egg whites too much.
Using a spoon or cookie scoop, scoop out portions of the coconut mixture and place them onto the prepared baking sheet, spacing them about 1 inch apart.
Flatten each portion slightly with the back of a spoon or your fingers to form small discs.
Bake in the preheated oven for 20-25 minutes, or until the edges of the cocadas are golden brown and the tops are lightly toasted.
Remove the baking sheet from the oven and let the cocadas cool completely on the pan.
Once cooled, carefully remove the cocadas from the baking sheet and transfer them to a wire rack to cool completely.
Store the cocadas in an airtight container at room temperature for up to a week.

These homemade cocadas are sweet, chewy, and full of coconut flavor. They make a delicious treat for any occasion and are perfect for sharing with family and friends. Enjoy!

Pineapple Empanadas

Ingredients:

For the Dough:

- 2 cups all-purpose flour
- 1/4 cup granulated sugar
- 1/2 teaspoon salt
- 1/2 cup unsalted butter, cold and cut into small cubes
- 1 large egg
- 2-3 tablespoons cold water

For the Filling:

- 2 cups diced pineapple (fresh or canned)
- 1/4 cup granulated sugar (adjust to taste depending on sweetness of pineapple)
- 1 tablespoon cornstarch
- 1 tablespoon lemon juice
- 1/2 teaspoon ground cinnamon
- Pinch of salt

For Assembly:

- 1 egg, beaten (for egg wash)
- Granulated sugar, for sprinkling (optional)

Instructions:

Preheat your oven to 375°F (190°C). Line a baking sheet with parchment paper. In a large mixing bowl, combine the flour, sugar, and salt. Add the cold butter cubes and use a pastry cutter or your fingers to cut the butter into the flour mixture until it resembles coarse crumbs.
In a small bowl, beat the egg with 2 tablespoons of cold water. Gradually add the beaten egg mixture to the flour mixture, mixing until the dough comes together. Add more water if needed, 1 tablespoon at a time.

Turn the dough out onto a lightly floured surface and knead it gently a few times until smooth. Wrap the dough in plastic wrap and refrigerate for at least 30 minutes.

Meanwhile, prepare the pineapple filling. In a saucepan, combine the diced pineapple, sugar, cornstarch, lemon juice, cinnamon, and salt. Cook over medium heat, stirring occasionally, until the mixture thickens, about 5-7 minutes. Remove from heat and let it cool completely.

Once the dough and filling are ready, roll out the dough on a floured surface to about 1/8 inch thickness. Use a round cutter or a small bowl to cut out circles of dough, about 4-5 inches in diameter.

Place a spoonful of the cooled pineapple filling in the center of each dough circle, leaving a border around the edges.

Fold the dough over the filling to create a half-moon shape and seal the edges by pressing with a fork or your fingers. Trim any excess dough if needed.

Transfer the filled empanadas to the prepared baking sheet. Brush the tops of the empanadas with beaten egg and sprinkle with granulated sugar, if desired.

Bake in the preheated oven for 20-25 minutes, or until the empanadas are golden brown.

Remove from the oven and let the empanadas cool slightly before serving.

These pineapple empanadas are best enjoyed warm or at room temperature. They're a delicious treat with a sweet and tangy pineapple filling wrapped in a flaky pastry crust. Enjoy them as a dessert or snack any time of day!

Alfajores (Dulce de Leche Sandwich Cookies)

Ingredients:

For the Cookies:

- 1 cup unsalted butter, softened
- 1/2 cup granulated sugar
- 2 large egg yolks
- 1 teaspoon vanilla extract
- 2 cups all-purpose flour
- 1/2 cup cornstarch
- 1/4 teaspoon salt

For Filling and Assembly:

- 1 cup dulce de leche
- Shredded coconut or powdered sugar, for coating (optional)

Instructions:

In a large mixing bowl, cream together the softened butter and granulated sugar until light and fluffy.
Add the egg yolks and vanilla extract to the butter mixture, and beat until well combined.
In a separate bowl, whisk together the flour, cornstarch, and salt.
Gradually add the dry ingredients to the wet ingredients, mixing until a soft dough forms. Be careful not to overmix.
Shape the dough into a ball, flatten it into a disk, wrap it in plastic wrap, and refrigerate for at least 30 minutes to firm up.
Preheat your oven to 350°F (175°C). Line a baking sheet with parchment paper.
On a lightly floured surface, roll out the chilled dough to about 1/4 inch thickness. Use a round cookie cutter to cut out cookies. Re-roll the scraps and continue cutting until all the dough is used.
Place the cookies on the prepared baking sheet and bake in the preheated oven for 10-12 minutes, or until the edges are lightly golden.
Remove the cookies from the oven and let them cool on the baking sheet for a few minutes before transferring them to a wire rack to cool completely.

Once the cookies are cooled, spread a generous amount of dulce de leche onto the bottom side of half of the cookies.

Top each dulce de leche-covered cookie with another cookie to create a sandwich.

Roll the edges of the sandwich cookies in shredded coconut or dust them with powdered sugar, if desired, for decoration.

Serve the alfajores at room temperature and enjoy!

These homemade alfajores are tender, buttery, and filled with rich dulce de leche, making them a perfect sweet treat for any occasion. Enjoy the delicious combination of flavors and textures in every bite!

Mexican Fruit Salad with Chili Powder

Ingredients:

- 2 cups diced pineapple
- 2 cups diced mango
- 2 cups diced watermelon
- 1 cup diced jicama
- 1 cup sliced strawberries
- 1/4 cup fresh lime juice
- 1-2 tablespoons honey or agave syrup (optional, for added sweetness)
- 1 teaspoon chili powder (such as Tajin or Ancho chili powder)
- Pinch of salt
- Fresh mint leaves, for garnish (optional)

Instructions:

In a large mixing bowl, combine the diced pineapple, mango, watermelon, jicama, and sliced strawberries.
In a small bowl, whisk together the fresh lime juice, honey or agave syrup (if using), chili powder, and a pinch of salt.
Pour the lime juice mixture over the fruit in the large mixing bowl.
Gently toss the fruit salad until all the fruits are evenly coated with the lime juice mixture.
Taste the fruit salad and adjust the seasoning, adding more chili powder or salt if desired.
Cover the bowl with plastic wrap or transfer the fruit salad to an airtight container, and refrigerate for at least 30 minutes to allow the flavors to meld together.
Before serving, give the fruit salad a final toss to redistribute the juices.
Garnish the Mexican Fruit Salad with fresh mint leaves, if desired, for a pop of color and extra freshness.
Serve the fruit salad chilled as a refreshing side dish or dessert.

This Mexican Fruit Salad with Chili Powder is bursting with vibrant colors, flavors, and textures, making it a perfect addition to any summer gathering or barbecue. Enjoy the sweet and spicy combination of fruits for a refreshing and satisfying treat!

Atole (Mexican Hot Cornmeal Drink)

Ingredients:

- 4 cups water or milk (or a combination of both)
- 1/2 cup masa harina (corn flour)
- 1/2 cup granulated sugar (adjust to taste)
- 1 cinnamon stick or 1 teaspoon ground cinnamon (optional)
- 1 teaspoon vanilla extract (optional)
- Pinch of salt

Instructions:

In a medium saucepan, combine the water or milk with the cinnamon stick (if using) and bring it to a gentle simmer over medium heat.

In a separate bowl, mix the masa harina with a little bit of cold water to form a smooth paste, ensuring there are no lumps.

Gradually whisk the masa harina paste into the simmering liquid, stirring constantly to prevent any lumps from forming.

Continue to cook the mixture over medium heat, stirring frequently, until it thickens to your desired consistency. This usually takes about 10-15 minutes.

Once the atole has thickened, stir in the granulated sugar, vanilla extract (if using), and a pinch of salt. Taste and adjust the sweetness as needed by adding more sugar if desired.

Continue to cook the atole for a few more minutes, stirring occasionally, to allow the flavors to meld together.

Remove the cinnamon stick (if used) from the atole before serving.

Serve the atole hot in mugs or cups.

Atole can be enjoyed on its own as a comforting beverage or paired with traditional Mexican sweet breads like pan dulce. It's a versatile drink that can be customized with different flavorings according to your preferences. Enjoy this delicious and warming Mexican hot cornmeal drink!

Mazapan (Mexican Peanut Candy)

Ingredients:

- 2 cups raw peanuts (unsalted)
- 1 1/2 cups granulated sugar
- Pinch of salt (optional)

Instructions:

Preheat your oven to 350°F (175°C). Spread the raw peanuts in a single layer on a baking sheet.

Roast the peanuts in the preheated oven for 8-10 minutes, stirring occasionally, until they are fragrant and lightly golden brown. Be careful not to let them burn.

Remove the peanuts from the oven and let them cool completely.

Once the peanuts are cool, transfer them to a food processor or high-powered blender. Pulse the peanuts in short bursts until they are finely ground into a coarse powder. Be careful not to over-process, or they may turn into peanut butter.

In a large mixing bowl, combine the ground peanuts with the granulated sugar and a pinch of salt, if using.

Mix the ingredients together until well combined. The mixture should resemble a coarse, crumbly dough.

Divide the mixture into small portions and shape each portion into a round or oval-shaped candy, pressing firmly to compact the mixture.

You can also use Mazapan molds to shape the candies for a more traditional look.

Once all the candies are shaped, wrap each one individually in wax paper or cellophane to prevent them from sticking together.

Store the Mazapan candies in an airtight container at room temperature for up to two weeks.

Mazapan is a popular treat enjoyed throughout Mexico, especially during Dia de los Muertos (Day of the Dead) and other festive occasions. Its crumbly texture and rich peanut flavor make it a beloved candy for both children and adults. Enjoy these homemade Mazapan candies as a sweet and nostalgic treat!

Cinnamon Sugar Buñuelos

Ingredients:

For the Dough:

- 2 cups all-purpose flour
- 1 teaspoon baking powder
- 1/4 teaspoon salt
- 2 tablespoons granulated sugar
- 2 tablespoons unsalted butter, melted
- 2/3 cup warm water

For Frying:

- Vegetable oil, for frying

For Coating:

- 1/2 cup granulated sugar
- 1 tablespoon ground cinnamon

Instructions:

In a large mixing bowl, combine the flour, baking powder, salt, and granulated sugar.

Add the melted butter to the dry ingredients and mix until well combined.

Gradually add the warm water to the flour mixture, mixing until a smooth dough forms. You may need to adjust the amount of water slightly to achieve the right consistency. The dough should be soft and pliable, but not too sticky.

Turn the dough out onto a lightly floured surface and knead it for a few minutes until smooth. Cover the dough with a clean kitchen towel and let it rest for about 30 minutes.

After the dough has rested, divide it into smaller portions and roll each portion out into a thin circle, about 1/8 inch thick.

Heat vegetable oil in a deep skillet or frying pan over medium-high heat until it reaches about 350°F (175°C).

Carefully place a piece of rolled-out dough into the hot oil, frying it until it puffs up and turns golden brown on one side, about 1-2 minutes. Then, flip it over and fry the other side until golden brown.

Once cooked, remove the buñuelo from the oil using a slotted spoon or tongs and drain it on paper towels to remove excess oil.

Repeat the frying process with the remaining pieces of dough, being careful not to overcrowd the pan.

In a shallow dish, mix together the granulated sugar and ground cinnamon for coating.

While the buñuelos are still warm, roll them in the cinnamon sugar mixture until completely coated.

Serve the cinnamon sugar buñuelos warm or at room temperature.

Cinnamon Sugar Buñuelos are best enjoyed fresh and warm, with their crispy exterior and sweet cinnamon sugar coating. They make a delightful dessert or snack that's sure to be a hit with family and friends!

Caramel Flan

Ingredients:

For the Caramel:

- 1 cup granulated sugar
- 1/4 cup water

For the Flan Custard:

- 4 large eggs
- 1 can (14 ounces) sweetened condensed milk
- 1 can (12 ounces) evaporated milk
- 1 teaspoon vanilla extract

Instructions:

Preheat your oven to 350°F (175°C). Place a large roasting pan filled with about 1 inch of hot water on the bottom rack of the oven. This will create a water bath for baking the flan.
To make the caramel, place the granulated sugar and water in a heavy-bottomed saucepan over medium heat. Swirl the pan gently to dissolve the sugar.
Allow the sugar to cook without stirring until it turns a deep amber color, about 8-10 minutes. Watch it closely to prevent burning.
Once the caramel reaches the desired color, immediately pour it into the bottom of a 9-inch round cake pan or flan mold, swirling to coat the bottom evenly. Be careful, as the caramel will be very hot.
In a large mixing bowl, whisk together the eggs, sweetened condensed milk, evaporated milk, and vanilla extract until well combined and smooth.
Pour the custard mixture over the caramel layer in the cake pan or flan mold.
Cover the cake pan or flan mold tightly with aluminum foil.
Place the cake pan or flan mold inside a larger baking dish and place it in the preheated oven, on the rack above the water-filled roasting pan.
Bake the flan for 50-60 minutes, or until the center is set but still slightly jiggly.
Carefully remove the flan from the oven and let it cool to room temperature.
Once cooled, refrigerate the flan for at least 4 hours, or preferably overnight, to chill and set completely.

To serve, run a knife around the edge of the flan to loosen it from the sides of the pan or mold. Place a serving plate upside down on top of the pan or mold, then quickly invert the flan onto the plate. The caramel sauce will flow over the top of the flan.

Slice the flan and serve chilled.

Caramel Flan is a creamy, indulgent dessert with a rich caramel flavor that's sure to impress your guests. Enjoy its silky texture and sweet taste as the perfect ending to any meal!

Arroz con Leche (Mexican Rice Pudding)

Ingredients:

- 1 cup long-grain white rice
- 4 cups whole milk
- 1 cinnamon stick
- 1/2 cup granulated sugar (adjust to taste)
- 1 teaspoon vanilla extract
- Pinch of salt
- Ground cinnamon, for garnish (optional)
- Raisins (optional)

Instructions:

Rinse the rice under cold water until the water runs clear. This helps remove excess starch from the rice.

In a large saucepan, combine the rinsed rice, milk, and cinnamon stick. Bring to a gentle boil over medium heat, then reduce the heat to low and simmer, stirring occasionally to prevent sticking, for about 30-35 minutes or until the rice is tender and the mixture has thickened.

Once the rice is cooked, add the sugar, vanilla extract, and a pinch of salt to the saucepan. Stir well to combine.

Continue to cook the mixture over low heat, stirring frequently, for another 10-15 minutes until the sugar has dissolved completely and the pudding has reached your desired consistency. It should be creamy and thick.

Remove the cinnamon stick from the rice pudding and discard it.

If using raisins, you can stir them into the rice pudding at this point.

Remove the saucepan from the heat and let the rice pudding cool slightly.

Transfer the rice pudding to serving bowls or glasses. You can serve it warm, at room temperature, or chilled, according to your preference.

Optionally, sprinkle ground cinnamon on top of each serving for garnish.

Serve the Arroz con Leche as is, or enjoy it with additional toppings such as fresh fruit or whipped cream.

Arroz con Leche is a comforting and delicious dessert that is perfect for any occasion. Its creamy texture and subtle sweetness make it a beloved treat in Mexican cuisine. Enjoy this classic dish with family and friends!

Bionico (Mexican Fruit Salad)

Ingredients:

For the Fruit Salad:

- 2 cups diced fresh pineapple
- 2 cups diced fresh mango
- 2 cups diced fresh papaya
- 2 cups diced fresh strawberries
- 1 cup diced fresh banana
- 1 cup diced fresh apple
- 1 cup diced fresh kiwi
- 1 cup diced fresh jicama (optional, for crunch)

For the Sauce:

- 1 cup plain yogurt
- 1/2 cup sweetened condensed milk
- 1 teaspoon vanilla extract
- Juice of 1 lime (optional, for tanginess)

For Serving:

- Granola
- Shredded coconut
- Chopped nuts (such as almonds or walnuts)
- Honey or agave syrup (optional, for extra sweetness)

Instructions:

In a large mixing bowl, combine all the diced fruits for the fruit salad. Mix well to combine.
In a separate bowl, whisk together the plain yogurt, sweetened condensed milk, vanilla extract, and lime juice (if using) to make the sauce.
Pour the sauce over the mixed fruits and gently toss until all the fruits are evenly coated with the sauce.

Cover the bowl with plastic wrap and refrigerate for at least 30 minutes to allow the flavors to meld together and the fruit salad to chill.

Before serving, divide the fruit salad into individual serving bowls or glasses.

Top each serving of fruit salad with a generous sprinkling of granola, shredded coconut, and chopped nuts.

Drizzle honey or agave syrup over the top, if desired, for extra sweetness.

Serve the Bionico immediately and enjoy!

Bionico is a delightful and customizable dessert that can be enjoyed any time of the day. Its combination of fresh fruits, creamy sauce, and crunchy toppings makes it a refreshing and satisfying treat. Customize the fruit selection and toppings according to your preferences and enjoy this delicious Mexican fruit salad with family and friends!

Cinnamon Churro Cheesecake Bars

Ingredients:

For the Crust:

- 1 1/2 cups graham cracker crumbs
- 1/4 cup granulated sugar
- 1/2 cup unsalted butter, melted

For the Cheesecake Filling:

- 16 ounces (2 packages) cream cheese, softened
- 2/3 cup granulated sugar
- 2 large eggs
- 1 teaspoon vanilla extract

For the Cinnamon Sugar Topping:

- 1/4 cup granulated sugar
- 1 tablespoon ground cinnamon
- 1/4 cup unsalted butter, melted

Instructions:

Preheat your oven to 350°F (175°C). Grease or line a 9x9-inch baking pan with parchment paper, leaving some overhang for easy removal.
In a medium bowl, combine the graham cracker crumbs, 1/4 cup granulated sugar, and melted butter. Mix until the crumbs are evenly moistened.
Press the crumb mixture into the bottom of the prepared baking pan in an even layer. Use the back of a spoon or a flat-bottomed glass to press it down firmly.
In a large mixing bowl, beat the softened cream cheese and 2/3 cup granulated sugar until smooth and creamy.
Add the eggs one at a time, mixing well after each addition. Stir in the vanilla extract until fully incorporated.
Pour the cheesecake filling over the graham cracker crust in the baking pan, spreading it out evenly with a spatula.
In a small bowl, mix together 1/4 cup granulated sugar and ground cinnamon for the cinnamon sugar topping.

Drizzle the melted butter evenly over the cheesecake filling in the pan. Sprinkle the cinnamon sugar mixture on top.

Bake in the preheated oven for 35-40 minutes, or until the edges are set and the center is slightly jiggly.

Remove the pan from the oven and let the cheesecake bars cool completely at room temperature.

Once cooled, transfer the pan to the refrigerator and chill the cheesecake bars for at least 2 hours, or until firm.

Once chilled, use the parchment paper overhang to lift the cheesecake bars out of the pan. Cut them into squares or bars using a sharp knife.

Serve the Cinnamon Churro Cheesecake Bars chilled, and enjoy!

These Cinnamon Churro Cheesecake Bars are a delightful fusion of flavors and textures, with a crunchy graham cracker crust, creamy cheesecake filling, and sweet cinnamon sugar topping. They're perfect for any occasion and sure to be a hit with family and friends!

Mexican Chocolate Ice Cream

Ingredients:

- 2 cups heavy cream
- 1 cup whole milk
- 3/4 cup granulated sugar
- 4 ounces Mexican chocolate, chopped (or dark chocolate if Mexican chocolate is unavailable)
- 1 teaspoon ground cinnamon
- 1/4 teaspoon cayenne pepper (adjust to taste)
- Pinch of salt
- 4 large egg yolks
- 1 teaspoon vanilla extract

Instructions:

In a medium saucepan, combine the heavy cream, whole milk, granulated sugar, chopped Mexican chocolate, ground cinnamon, cayenne pepper, and a pinch of salt.

Place the saucepan over medium heat and stir occasionally until the mixture comes to a simmer and the chocolate is completely melted. Do not let it boil.

In a separate mixing bowl, whisk the egg yolks until smooth.

Gradually pour a small amount of the hot chocolate mixture into the bowl with the egg yolks, whisking constantly to temper the eggs.

Gradually add the tempered egg mixture back into the saucepan with the remaining hot chocolate mixture, whisking constantly.

Cook the mixture over medium heat, stirring constantly with a wooden spoon or heatproof spatula, until it thickens slightly and coats the back of the spoon, about 5-7 minutes. Do not let it boil.

Once thickened, remove the saucepan from the heat and strain the mixture through a fine-mesh sieve into a clean bowl to remove any lumps.

Stir in the vanilla extract until well combined.

Cover the bowl with plastic wrap, pressing it directly onto the surface of the custard to prevent a skin from forming. Chill the mixture in the refrigerator for at least 4 hours, or preferably overnight, until completely cold.

Once chilled, transfer the custard mixture to an ice cream maker and churn according to the manufacturer's instructions until it reaches a soft-serve consistency.

Transfer the churned ice cream to a freezer-safe container, cover it with a lid, and freeze for at least 4 hours, or until firm.
Serve the Mexican Chocolate Ice Cream scooped into bowls or cones, and enjoy!

This Mexican Chocolate Ice Cream is creamy, indulgent, and packed with delicious flavors that will surely satisfy your sweet tooth. Serve it on its own or with toppings like whipped cream, chocolate sauce, or chopped nuts for an extra special treat!

Mexican Wedding Cake (Pastel de Tres Leches)

Ingredients:

For the Cake:

- 1 cup all-purpose flour
- 1 1/2 teaspoons baking powder
- 1/4 teaspoon salt
- 5 large eggs, separated
- 1 cup granulated sugar, divided
- 1/3 cup whole milk
- 1 teaspoon vanilla extract

For the Tres Leches Mixture:

- 1 can (12 ounces) evaporated milk
- 1 can (14 ounces) sweetened condensed milk
- 1 cup heavy cream

For the Topping:

- 2 cups whipped cream
- Ground cinnamon or cinnamon sticks, for garnish (optional)

Instructions:

Preheat your oven to 350°F (175°C). Grease and flour a 9x13-inch baking dish.
In a medium bowl, sift together the flour, baking powder, and salt. Set aside.
In a large mixing bowl, beat the egg yolks with 3/4 cup of granulated sugar until pale and thick. Add the whole milk and vanilla extract, and mix until well combined.
Gradually add the sifted dry ingredients to the egg yolk mixture, stirring until smooth.
In a separate clean mixing bowl, beat the egg whites until soft peaks form. Gradually add the remaining 1/4 cup of granulated sugar, and continue to beat until stiff peaks form.

Gently fold the beaten egg whites into the cake batter until just combined. Be careful not to deflate the egg whites too much.

Pour the batter into the prepared baking dish and spread it out evenly.

Bake in the preheated oven for 25-30 minutes, or until a toothpick inserted into the center of the cake comes out clean.

While the cake is baking, prepare the Tres Leches mixture. In a large measuring cup or bowl, whisk together the evaporated milk, sweetened condensed milk, and heavy cream until well combined.

Once the cake is baked and while it's still warm, use a fork or skewer to poke holes all over the surface of the cake.

Slowly pour the Tres Leches mixture evenly over the warm cake, allowing it to absorb the liquid.

Cover the cake with plastic wrap and refrigerate for at least 4 hours, or preferably overnight, to allow the cake to soak up the Tres Leches mixture.

Before serving, spread whipped cream over the top of the cake.

Optionally, garnish with a sprinkle of ground cinnamon or cinnamon sticks for decoration.

Serve the Mexican Wedding Cake chilled and enjoy its moist and creamy texture!

This Mexican Wedding Cake, or Pastel de Tres Leches, is a luscious and indulgent dessert that's perfect for celebrating special occasions or simply treating yourself to a delicious sweet treat. Enjoy its rich flavor and creamy texture with family and friends!

Coconut Tres Leches Cake

Ingredients:

For the Cake:

- 1 cup all-purpose flour
- 1 1/2 teaspoons baking powder
- 1/4 teaspoon salt
- 5 large eggs, separated
- 1 cup granulated sugar, divided
- 1/3 cup coconut milk
- 1 teaspoon vanilla extract

For the Tres Leches Mixture:

- 1 can (12 ounces) evaporated milk
- 1 can (14 ounces) sweetened condensed milk
- 1 cup coconut milk

For the Whipped Cream Topping:

- 2 cups heavy cream
- 1/4 cup powdered sugar
- 1 teaspoon vanilla extract
- Sweetened shredded coconut, for garnish

Instructions:

Preheat your oven to 350°F (175°C). Grease and flour a 9x13-inch baking dish.
In a medium bowl, sift together the flour, baking powder, and salt. Set aside.
In a large mixing bowl, beat the egg yolks with 3/4 cup of granulated sugar until pale and thick. Add the coconut milk and vanilla extract, and mix until well combined.
Gradually add the sifted dry ingredients to the egg yolk mixture, stirring until smooth.
In a separate clean mixing bowl, beat the egg whites until soft peaks form. Gradually add the remaining 1/4 cup of granulated sugar, and continue to beat until stiff peaks form.

Gently fold the beaten egg whites into the cake batter until just combined. Be careful not to deflate the egg whites too much.

Pour the batter into the prepared baking dish and spread it out evenly.

Bake in the preheated oven for 25-30 minutes, or until a toothpick inserted into the center of the cake comes out clean.

While the cake is baking, prepare the Tres Leches mixture. In a large measuring cup or bowl, whisk together the evaporated milk, sweetened condensed milk, and coconut milk until well combined.

Once the cake is baked and while it's still warm, use a fork or skewer to poke holes all over the surface of the cake.

Slowly pour the Tres Leches mixture evenly over the warm cake, allowing it to absorb the liquid.

Cover the cake with plastic wrap and refrigerate for at least 4 hours, or preferably overnight, to allow the cake to soak up the Tres Leches mixture.

Before serving, prepare the whipped cream topping. In a mixing bowl, beat the heavy cream, powdered sugar, and vanilla extract until stiff peaks form.

Spread the whipped cream over the top of the chilled cake.

Sprinkle sweetened shredded coconut over the whipped cream topping for garnish.

Slice and serve the Coconut Tres Leches Cake chilled. Enjoy its tropical flavors and creamy texture!

This Coconut Tres Leches Cake is a delightful and indulgent dessert that's perfect for any occasion, especially for those who love coconut. Enjoy its rich flavor and moist texture with family and friends!

Mexican Hot Chocolate Brownies

Ingredients:

For the Brownies:

- 1/2 cup unsalted butter
- 1 cup granulated sugar
- 2 large eggs
- 1 teaspoon vanilla extract
- 1/3 cup unsweetened cocoa powder
- 1/2 cup all-purpose flour
- 1/4 teaspoon salt
- 1/2 teaspoon ground cinnamon
- 1/4 teaspoon cayenne pepper (optional, for a spicy kick)
- 1/4 teaspoon ground nutmeg

For the Topping:

- 1 tablespoon granulated sugar
- 1/2 teaspoon ground cinnamon

Instructions:

Preheat your oven to 350°F (175°C). Grease and flour an 8x8-inch baking pan or line it with parchment paper for easy removal.
In a medium saucepan, melt the butter over low heat. Remove from heat and let it cool slightly.
Stir in the granulated sugar, eggs, and vanilla extract into the melted butter until well combined.
In a separate bowl, sift together the cocoa powder, flour, salt, ground cinnamon, cayenne pepper (if using), and ground nutmeg.
Gradually add the dry ingredients to the wet ingredients, mixing until just combined. Do not overmix.
Pour the brownie batter into the prepared baking pan and spread it out evenly with a spatula.

In a small bowl, mix together the tablespoon of granulated sugar and half teaspoon of ground cinnamon for the topping.

Sprinkle the cinnamon-sugar mixture evenly over the top of the brownie batter.

Bake in the preheated oven for 20-25 minutes, or until a toothpick inserted into the center comes out with a few moist crumbs.

Remove the brownies from the oven and let them cool in the pan for about 10-15 minutes.

Once cooled, use a sharp knife to cut the brownies into squares.

Serve the Mexican Hot Chocolate Brownies warm or at room temperature.

These Mexican Hot Chocolate Brownies are rich, fudgy, and filled with warm spices that add a delightful twist to a classic dessert. Enjoy them with a glass of milk or a cup of hot chocolate for the ultimate indulgence!

Cinnamon Sugar Sopapilla Cheesecake Bars

Ingredients:

For the Cheesecake Filling:

- 16 ounces (2 packages) cream cheese, softened
- 1 cup granulated sugar
- 1 teaspoon vanilla extract
- 2 large eggs

For the Sopapilla Layer:

- 2 cans (8 ounces each) refrigerated crescent roll dough
- 1/2 cup unsalted butter, melted
- 1/2 cup granulated sugar
- 1 tablespoon ground cinnamon

Instructions:

Preheat your oven to 350°F (175°C). Grease a 9x13-inch baking dish.
In a large mixing bowl, beat the softened cream cheese, granulated sugar, and vanilla extract until smooth and creamy.
Add the eggs one at a time, beating well after each addition, until fully incorporated. Set aside.
Unroll one can of crescent roll dough and press it into the bottom of the prepared baking dish, making sure to seal any perforations in the dough.
Spread the prepared cheesecake filling evenly over the layer of crescent roll dough in the baking dish.
Unroll the second can of crescent roll dough and place it over the cheesecake filling, gently pressing down to adhere it to the filling and seal any perforations.
In a small bowl, mix together the granulated sugar and ground cinnamon for the sopapilla topping.
Drizzle the melted butter evenly over the top layer of crescent roll dough.
Sprinkle the cinnamon sugar mixture evenly over the melted butter.
Bake in the preheated oven for 30-35 minutes, or until the top is golden brown and the cheesecake layer is set.
Remove the baking dish from the oven and let it cool completely on a wire rack.

Once cooled, refrigerate the sopapilla cheesecake bars for at least 2 hours, or preferably overnight, to allow them to set.
Once chilled, slice the bars into squares or rectangles.
Serve the cinnamon sugar sopapilla cheesecake bars chilled or at room temperature.

These Cinnamon Sugar Sopapilla Cheesecake Bars are a delightful fusion of flavors and textures, with a creamy cheesecake filling sandwiched between layers of sweet and crispy sopapilla dough. Enjoy them as a delicious dessert for any occasion!

Mexican Chocolate Tiramisu

Ingredients:

- 1 cup heavy cream
- 1/2 cup granulated sugar
- 8 ounces mascarpone cheese, softened
- 1 teaspoon vanilla extract
- 1 tablespoon ground cinnamon
- 1/4 teaspoon cayenne pepper (optional, for a spicy kick)
- 1/4 cup coffee liqueur (such as Kahlua) or brewed espresso, cooled
- 1/4 cup milk
- 1/4 cup chocolate liqueur (such as Godiva) (optional)
- 1 package ladyfinger cookies (savoiardi)
- 1/4 cup unsweetened cocoa powder, for dusting
- Shaved chocolate or chocolate curls, for garnish (optional)

Instructions:

In a large mixing bowl, beat the heavy cream and granulated sugar together until stiff peaks form.
In another mixing bowl, combine the softened mascarpone cheese, vanilla extract, ground cinnamon, and cayenne pepper (if using). Mix until smooth and well combined.
Gently fold the whipped cream into the mascarpone mixture until fully incorporated. Set aside.
In a shallow dish, combine the coffee liqueur or brewed espresso, milk, and chocolate liqueur (if using).
Quickly dip each ladyfinger cookie into the coffee mixture, making sure not to soak them too long, as they will become too soggy.
Arrange a layer of dipped ladyfinger cookies in the bottom of a 9x9-inch square baking dish or a similar-sized serving dish.
Spread half of the mascarpone mixture evenly over the layer of ladyfingers.
Repeat the layers with another layer of dipped ladyfinger cookies followed by the remaining mascarpone mixture.
Cover the dish with plastic wrap and refrigerate for at least 4 hours, or preferably overnight, to allow the flavors to meld together and the tiramisu to set.
Before serving, dust the top of the tiramisu with unsweetened cocoa powder.

Optionally, garnish with shaved chocolate or chocolate curls for an elegant presentation.
Slice and serve the Mexican Chocolate Tiramisu chilled.

This Mexican Chocolate Tiramisu is a luxurious and decadent dessert that combines the flavors of creamy mascarpone cheese, rich chocolate, and warm spices for a truly unforgettable treat. Enjoy it with family and friends for a special occasion or any time you crave a delicious dessert!

Horchata (Mexican Rice Drink)

Ingredients:

- 1 cup long-grain white rice
- 4 cups water, divided
- 1 cinnamon stick
- 1/2 cup granulated sugar (adjust to taste)
- 1 teaspoon vanilla extract
- 2 cups whole milk or almond milk (for a dairy-free version)
- Ground cinnamon, for garnish (optional)

Instructions:

Rinse the rice under cold water until the water runs clear. This helps remove excess starch from the rice.

In a blender, combine the rinsed rice, 2 cups of water, and the cinnamon stick. Blend on high speed until the rice is broken down into fine particles, about 1-2 minutes.

Transfer the rice mixture to a large bowl and add the remaining 2 cups of water. Stir well to combine.

Cover the bowl and let the rice mixture soak at room temperature for at least 4 hours, or preferably overnight. This allows the flavors to meld together and the rice to soften.

Once the rice has soaked, remove the cinnamon stick from the mixture and discard it.

Working in batches, pour the rice mixture into a blender and blend until smooth.

Strain the blended rice mixture through a fine-mesh sieve or cheesecloth into a pitcher to remove any remaining solids. Press down on the solids to extract as much liquid as possible.

Stir in the granulated sugar and vanilla extract until the sugar is fully dissolved.

If using whole milk, stir it into the horchata mixture until well combined. If using almond milk or another dairy-free alternative, you can add it directly to the pitcher.

Refrigerate the horchata for at least 1 hour, or until chilled.

Before serving, stir the horchata well to ensure the flavors are evenly distributed.

Pour the horchata into glasses filled with ice cubes.

Optionally, sprinkle ground cinnamon on top of each serving for garnish.

Serve the horchata cold and enjoy its creamy, refreshing flavor!

Horchata is a delicious and satisfying beverage that's easy to make at home. Enjoy it as a refreshing treat on its own or paired with your favorite Mexican dishes for a truly authentic culinary experience!

Tamarind Candy (Mexican Dulce de Tamarindo)

Ingredients:

- 1 cup tamarind pulp (seedless)
- 1 cup granulated sugar
- 1/4 cup water
- Pinch of salt
- Chili powder (optional, for a spicy kick)

Instructions:

Remove any seeds from the tamarind pulp and place it in a bowl.
In a small saucepan, combine the granulated sugar, water, and a pinch of salt.
Heat the mixture over medium heat, stirring occasionally, until the sugar is completely dissolved and the mixture comes to a simmer.
Once the sugar has dissolved, pour the hot sugar syrup over the tamarind pulp in the bowl.
Let the tamarind pulp soak in the sugar syrup for about 30 minutes, allowing the flavors to meld together.
After soaking, use a fork or a potato masher to mash the tamarind pulp and mix it well with the sugar syrup until you get a smooth paste-like consistency.
If desired, you can add a pinch of chili powder to the mixture for a spicy flavor.
Line a baking sheet or tray with parchment paper.
Scoop out small portions of the tamarind mixture and roll them into balls or shape them into small discs using your hands.
Place the shaped tamarind candies on the prepared baking sheet and let them dry at room temperature for several hours, or until they are firm to the touch.
Once dry, you can store the tamarind candies in an airtight container at room temperature for up to several weeks.

Enjoy these homemade Mexican Dulce de Tamarindo candies as a sweet and tangy treat any time you crave a burst of flavor! They're perfect for satisfying your sweet tooth with a hint of tropical flair.

Coconut Flan

Ingredients:

For the Caramel:

- 1 cup granulated sugar
- 1/4 cup water

For the Flan:

- 1 can (14 ounces) sweetened condensed milk
- 1 can (13.5 ounces) coconut milk
- 1 cup coconut cream
- 5 large eggs
- 1 teaspoon vanilla extract
- 1/2 cup sweetened shredded coconut (optional, for added texture)

Instructions:

Preheat your oven to 350°F (175°C). Prepare a 9-inch round cake pan or flan mold by greasing it lightly with butter.

To make the caramel, place the granulated sugar and water in a saucepan over medium heat. Stir until the sugar is dissolved.

Allow the mixture to cook without stirring until it turns a deep amber color, about 8-10 minutes. Swirl the pan occasionally to ensure even caramelization.

Once the caramel reaches the desired color, immediately pour it into the prepared cake pan, tilting the pan to coat the bottom evenly. Be careful as the caramel will be very hot. Set aside to cool and harden.

In a blender, combine the sweetened condensed milk, coconut milk, coconut cream, eggs, and vanilla extract. Blend until smooth and well combined.

If using sweetened shredded coconut, sprinkle it evenly over the cooled caramel layer in the cake pan.

Carefully pour the flan mixture over the caramel layer in the cake pan.

Place the cake pan inside a larger baking dish or roasting pan. Fill the larger dish with hot water until it reaches halfway up the sides of the cake pan. This water bath will help the flan cook evenly and prevent cracking.

Transfer the baking dish to the preheated oven and bake for 50-60 minutes, or until the edges are set but the center still jiggles slightly when shaken.

Once baked, remove the flan from the oven and let it cool to room temperature. Then, cover and refrigerate for at least 4 hours, or preferably overnight, to allow it to set completely.

To serve, run a knife around the edges of the flan to loosen it from the pan. Place a serving plate upside down over the pan and carefully invert the flan onto the plate, allowing the caramel to flow over the top.

Slice and serve the coconut flan chilled. Enjoy the creamy texture and tropical flavor!

This coconut flan is a decadent and refreshing dessert that's perfect for any occasion, especially for those who love the tropical taste of coconut. It's sure to impress your family and friends with its creamy texture and rich flavor.

Cajeta Crepes

Ingredients:

For the Crepes:

- 1 cup all-purpose flour
- 2 large eggs
- 1 cup milk
- 2 tablespoons unsalted butter, melted
- 1 tablespoon granulated sugar
- 1/4 teaspoon salt
- Butter or oil for cooking

For the Cajeta Filling:

- 1 cup cajeta (store-bought or homemade)
- 1 tablespoon unsalted butter

For Serving:

- Powdered sugar (optional)
- Fresh berries or sliced fruit (optional)

Instructions:

1. Make the Crepe Batter:

    In a blender, combine the flour, eggs, milk, melted butter, sugar, and salt. Blend until smooth and well combined. Alternatively, you can whisk the ingredients together in a mixing bowl until smooth.
    Let the batter rest for about 15-30 minutes at room temperature to allow the gluten to relax.

2. Cook the Crepes:

    Heat a non-stick skillet or crepe pan over medium heat. Lightly grease the skillet with butter or oil.

Pour about 1/4 cup of the crepe batter into the skillet, swirling it around to evenly coat the bottom. Cook for about 1-2 minutes, or until the edges start to lift and the bottom is lightly golden brown.

Carefully flip the crepe using a spatula and cook for an additional 1-2 minutes on the other side, until lightly golden brown. Transfer the cooked crepe to a plate and cover with a clean kitchen towel to keep warm. Repeat with the remaining batter, greasing the skillet as needed.

3. Prepare the Cajeta Filling:

In a small saucepan, heat the cajeta and unsalted butter over low heat until warm and smooth. Stir occasionally to prevent burning. Remove from heat.

4. Assemble the Cajeta Crepes:

Place a cooked crepe on a serving plate. Spoon a generous amount of warm cajeta filling onto one half of the crepe.

Fold the crepe in half over the filling, then fold it in half again to form a triangle or roll it up into a cylinder.

Repeat with the remaining crepes and cajeta filling.

5. Serve:

Dust the cajeta crepes with powdered sugar, if desired.

Serve the crepes warm, garnished with fresh berries or sliced fruit, if desired.

Enjoy these delicious cajeta crepes as a decadent dessert or special breakfast treat!

These cajeta crepes are sure to impress with their rich and creamy caramel flavor. Whether served as a dessert or breakfast, they are a delightful indulgence that will please any crowd.

Chocolate Tamale

Ingredients:

For the Chocolate Dough:

- 2 cups masa harina (corn flour for tamales)
- 1/2 cup unsweetened cocoa powder
- 1/2 teaspoon baking powder
- 1/2 teaspoon salt
- 3/4 cup granulated sugar
- 1/2 cup unsalted butter, softened
- 1 1/2 cups warm water or vegetable broth

For the Filling:

- 1 cup semi-sweet chocolate chips or chopped chocolate
- 1/2 cup heavy cream
- 2 tablespoons granulated sugar
- 1 teaspoon vanilla extract

For Assembling the Tamales:

- Dried corn husks, soaked in warm water for at least 30 minutes and drained
- Kitchen twine or strips of soaked corn husks for tying

Instructions:

1. Prepare the Chocolate Dough:

> In a large mixing bowl, combine the masa harina, cocoa powder, baking powder, salt, and granulated sugar. Mix well to combine.
> Add the softened butter to the dry ingredients and mix until the mixture resembles coarse crumbs.
> Gradually pour in the warm water or vegetable broth, mixing with your hands until a smooth, slightly sticky dough forms. Cover the dough and set it aside while you prepare the filling.

2. Make the Chocolate Filling:

   In a small saucepan, heat the heavy cream over medium heat until it begins to simmer.
   Remove the saucepan from the heat and add the chocolate chips or chopped chocolate, granulated sugar, and vanilla extract to the hot cream. Let it sit for 1-2 minutes.
   Stir the chocolate mixture until the chocolate is completely melted and smooth. Set aside to cool slightly.

3. Assemble the Chocolate Tamales:

   Take a soaked corn husk and spread about 2 tablespoons of the chocolate dough onto the wide end of the husk, leaving a border around the edges.
   Spoon a tablespoon of the chocolate filling down the center of the dough.
   Fold one side of the corn husk over the filling, then fold the other side over to enclose the filling completely.
   Fold the bottom end of the corn husk up to seal the tamale, then tie it securely with kitchen twine or a strip of soaked corn husk.
   Repeat the process with the remaining dough and filling.

4. Steam the Chocolate Tamales:

   Arrange the assembled tamales vertically in a steamer basket, open-side up, making sure they are tightly packed to prevent unraveling.
   Cover the tamales with a damp kitchen towel or additional soaked corn husks, then cover the steamer with a lid.
   Steam the tamales over simmering water for 1 to 1 1/2 hours, or until the dough is firm and cooked through.
   Check the tamales occasionally and add more water to the steamer if needed.
   Once cooked, remove the tamales from the steamer and let them cool for a few minutes before serving.

5. Serve the Chocolate Tamales:

   Unwrap the tamales from the corn husks and serve them warm.

Optionally, garnish the tamales with powdered sugar, chocolate sauce, whipped cream, or fresh berries before serving.
Enjoy these delicious chocolate tamales as a special dessert or sweet treat!

These chocolate tamales are a delightful twist on traditional tamales and are sure to be a hit at any gathering. The combination of rich chocolate dough and creamy chocolate filling makes for a decadent and satisfying dessert experience.

Pineapple Upside Down Cake with a Twist

Ingredients:

For the Pineapple Layer:

- 1/4 cup unsalted butter
- 1/2 cup packed brown sugar
- 1 can (20 ounces) pineapple slices in juice, drained (reserve juice)
- Maraschino cherries, drained

For the Cake Batter:

- 1 1/2 cups all-purpose flour
- 1 cup granulated sugar
- 1/2 cup unsalted butter, softened
- 2 large eggs
- 1 teaspoon vanilla extract
- 1/2 cup reserved pineapple juice (from the canned pineapple)
- 2 teaspoons baking powder
- 1/4 teaspoon salt

Instructions:

Preheat your oven to 350°F (175°C). Grease a 9-inch round cake pan or a similar-sized baking dish.

Prepare the Pineapple Layer:
- Melt the 1/4 cup of butter in a saucepan over medium heat.
- Stir in the brown sugar until it's dissolved and forms a caramel-like mixture.
- Pour the mixture into the bottom of the prepared cake pan, spreading it out evenly.
- Arrange the pineapple slices on top of the caramel mixture, placing a maraschino cherry in the center of each pineapple slice.

Prepare the Cake Batter:
- In a mixing bowl, cream together the softened butter and granulated sugar until light and fluffy.

- Add the eggs one at a time, beating well after each addition. Stir in the vanilla extract.
- In a separate bowl, sift together the flour, baking powder, and salt.
- Gradually add the dry ingredients to the butter mixture, alternating with the reserved pineapple juice, and mixing until well combined.

Pour the cake batter over the pineapple layer in the cake pan, spreading it out evenly.

Bake in the preheated oven for 40-45 minutes, or until a toothpick inserted into the center of the cake comes out clean.

Allow the cake to cool in the pan for about 10 minutes.

Once cooled slightly, carefully invert the cake onto a serving plate. Leave the pan on top of the cake for a few minutes to allow the caramel to drizzle over the cake.

Carefully remove the cake pan and let the cake cool completely before serving.

Slice and serve the Pineapple Upside Down Cake with a Twist, garnishing with additional maraschino cherries or whipped cream if desired.

This Pineapple Upside Down Cake with a Twist is a delicious variation of the classic dessert, with the addition of a rich caramel layer and a moist and flavorful cake. Enjoy its tropical flavors and unique presentation!

Mexican Mango Ice Cream (Nieve de Mango)

Ingredients:

- 3 ripe mangoes, peeled, pitted, and chopped
- 1 can (14 ounces) sweetened condensed milk
- 1 cup whole milk or heavy cream
- 1/4 cup granulated sugar (optional, adjust to taste)
- 1 teaspoon vanilla extract
- Juice of 1 lime (optional, for added freshness)

Instructions:

In a blender or food processor, combine the chopped mangoes, sweetened condensed milk, whole milk or heavy cream, granulated sugar (if using), vanilla extract, and lime juice (if using). Blend until smooth and creamy.
Taste the mixture and adjust the sweetness level by adding more sugar if desired.
Pour the mango mixture into a shallow dish or baking pan. Cover with plastic wrap and freeze for about 2-3 hours, or until the edges start to set.
Remove the pan from the freezer and use a fork or spoon to scrape and stir the partially frozen mixture, breaking up any ice crystals. Return the pan to the freezer.
Repeat this process every 30 minutes for about 2-3 hours, or until the mango ice cream is uniformly frozen and creamy.
Once the ice cream reaches the desired consistency, transfer it to a lidded container and freeze for an additional 1-2 hours to firm up.
Serve the Mexican Mango Ice Cream (Nieve de Mango) scooped into bowls or cones. Garnish with fresh mango slices or mint leaves if desired.
Enjoy this refreshing and creamy mango ice cream on its own or as a topping for other desserts.

This homemade Mexican Mango Ice Cream is bursting with tropical flavor and is sure to be a hit with mango lovers of all ages. It's a perfect way to cool down and enjoy the sweetness of ripe mangoes during the summer months.

Sopaipilla Cheesecake Bars

Ingredients:

For the Cheesecake Filling:

- 16 ounces cream cheese, softened
- 1 cup granulated sugar
- 1 teaspoon vanilla extract
- 2 large eggs

For the Sopaipilla Dough:

- 2 cans (8 ounces each) refrigerated crescent roll dough

For the Topping:

- 1/4 cup granulated sugar
- 1 teaspoon ground cinnamon
- 1/4 cup unsalted butter, melted

Instructions:

Preheat your oven to 350°F (175°C). Grease a 9x13-inch baking dish.
In a mixing bowl, beat the softened cream cheese until smooth.
Add the granulated sugar and vanilla extract to the cream cheese, and beat until well combined.
Add the eggs, one at a time, beating well after each addition, until the mixture is smooth and creamy. Set aside.
Unroll one can of crescent roll dough and press it into the bottom of the prepared baking dish, making sure to seal any perforations in the dough.
Spread the prepared cheesecake filling evenly over the layer of crescent roll dough in the baking dish.
Unroll the second can of crescent roll dough and place it over the cheesecake filling, gently pressing down to adhere it to the filling and seal any perforations.
In a small bowl, mix together the granulated sugar and ground cinnamon for the topping.

Drizzle the melted butter evenly over the top layer of crescent roll dough.
Sprinkle the cinnamon-sugar mixture evenly over the melted butter.
Bake in the preheated oven for 25-30 minutes, or until the top is golden brown and the cheesecake layer is set.
Remove the baking dish from the oven and let it cool completely on a wire rack.
Once cooled, refrigerate the sopaipilla cheesecake bars for at least 4 hours, or preferably overnight, to allow them to set.
Once chilled, slice the bars into squares or rectangles.
Serve the Sopaipilla Cheesecake Bars chilled or at room temperature.

These Sopaipilla Cheesecake Bars are a delightful fusion of flavors and textures, with a creamy cheesecake filling sandwiched between layers of sweet and crispy sopaipilla dough. Enjoy them as a delicious dessert for any occasion!

Mexican Chocolate Mousse

Ingredients:

- 6 ounces (170g) Mexican chocolate, chopped
- 1/4 cup (60ml) water
- 3 large eggs, separated
- 1/4 cup (50g) granulated sugar
- 1 teaspoon vanilla extract
- 1 cup (240ml) heavy cream
- Whipped cream, for garnish (optional)
- Shaved chocolate, for garnish (optional)

Instructions:

Place the chopped Mexican chocolate and water in a heatproof bowl set over a pot of simmering water (double boiler). Stir occasionally until the chocolate is melted and smooth. Remove from heat and let it cool slightly.

In a separate bowl, beat the egg yolks with the granulated sugar until pale and thickened. Stir in the vanilla extract.

Gradually whisk the melted chocolate into the egg yolk mixture until well combined. Set aside.

In another bowl, whip the heavy cream until stiff peaks form.

In a clean, dry bowl, beat the egg whites until stiff peaks form.

Gently fold the whipped cream into the chocolate mixture until well combined and no streaks remain.

Then, carefully fold in the beaten egg whites until fully incorporated, being careful not to deflate the mixture.

Divide the mousse evenly among serving dishes or glasses.

Cover and refrigerate the mousse for at least 2 hours, or until set.

Before serving, garnish with whipped cream and shaved chocolate, if desired.

Serve chilled and enjoy the rich and creamy Mexican Chocolate Mousse!

This Mexican Chocolate Mousse is decadent, creamy, and has a hint of spice from the Mexican chocolate, making it a delightful dessert for any occasion. Enjoy!

Buñuelos de Viento (Mexican Wind Fritters)

Ingredients:

For the Dough:

- 1 cup water
- 1/4 cup unsalted butter
- 1 tablespoon granulated sugar
- 1/4 teaspoon salt
- 1 cup all-purpose flour
- 4 large eggs

For Frying:

- Vegetable oil, for frying

For Coating:

- 1/2 cup granulated sugar
- 1 teaspoon ground cinnamon

Instructions:

In a medium saucepan, combine the water, butter, sugar, and salt. Bring the mixture to a boil over medium heat, stirring occasionally.
Once the mixture reaches a boil, remove it from the heat and add the flour all at once. Stir vigorously until the mixture forms a smooth dough.
Return the saucepan to the heat and continue to cook the dough, stirring constantly, for about 1-2 minutes to slightly dry it out.
Transfer the dough to a mixing bowl and let it cool for a few minutes.
Beat in the eggs, one at a time, mixing well after each addition, until the dough is smooth and glossy.
Heat vegetable oil in a deep skillet or pot to 350°F (175°C).
Drop spoonfuls of dough into the hot oil, frying in batches to avoid overcrowding, until the buñuelos are golden brown and puffed up, about 2-3 minutes per side.

Use a slotted spoon to transfer the fried buñuelos to a plate lined with paper towels to drain excess oil.

In a shallow dish, mix together the granulated sugar and ground cinnamon for the coating.

While the buñuelos are still warm, roll them in the cinnamon sugar mixture to coat evenly.

Serve the buñuelos de viento warm or at room temperature.

Enjoy these delicious Mexican Wind Fritters as a sweet and crispy treat!

Buñuelos de viento are best enjoyed fresh, but you can store any leftovers in an airtight container at room temperature for up to a day. Just reheat them in the oven before serving to restore their crispiness.

Mexican Coconut Lime Bars

Ingredients:

For the Crust:

- 1 1/2 cups graham cracker crumbs
- 1/4 cup granulated sugar
- 1/2 cup unsalted butter, melted

For the Coconut Lime Filling:

- 1 can (14 ounces) sweetened condensed milk
- 1/2 cup coconut milk
- Zest of 2 limes
- 1/2 cup lime juice (about 4-5 limes)
- 4 large egg yolks
- 1 cup sweetened shredded coconut

For Garnish (optional):

- Powdered sugar
- Lime slices
- Toasted shredded coconut

Instructions:

Preheat your oven to 350°F (175°C). Grease or line a 9x9-inch baking pan with parchment paper.
In a mixing bowl, combine the graham cracker crumbs, granulated sugar, and melted butter for the crust. Mix until well combined.
Press the crumb mixture evenly into the bottom of the prepared baking pan.
Bake the crust in the preheated oven for 8-10 minutes, or until lightly golden brown. Remove from the oven and let it cool slightly.
While the crust is cooling, prepare the coconut lime filling. In a separate mixing bowl, whisk together the sweetened condensed milk, coconut milk, lime zest, lime juice, and egg yolks until smooth.

Stir in the sweetened shredded coconut until evenly distributed.

Pour the coconut lime filling over the partially baked crust, spreading it out evenly.

Return the baking pan to the oven and bake for an additional 20-25 minutes, or until the filling is set and the edges are lightly golden brown.

Remove the baking pan from the oven and let the bars cool completely at room temperature.

Once cooled, refrigerate the bars for at least 2 hours, or until chilled and firm.

Once chilled, use a sharp knife to cut the bars into squares or rectangles.

Garnish the bars with powdered sugar, lime slices, and toasted shredded coconut, if desired, before serving.

Serve these delicious Mexican Coconut Lime Bars chilled and enjoy their refreshing tropical flavor!

These bars are a delightful combination of sweet coconut and tangy lime, perfect for any occasion. They're sure to be a hit at parties, potlucks, or as a special treat for yourself and your loved ones.

Chocolate Abuelita Cupcakes

Ingredients:

For the Cupcakes:

- 1 cup all-purpose flour
- 1/2 cup unsweetened cocoa powder
- 1 teaspoon baking powder
- 1/2 teaspoon baking soda
- 1/4 teaspoon salt
- 2 Abuelita chocolate tablets, finely chopped
- 1/2 cup unsalted butter, softened
- 1 cup granulated sugar
- 2 large eggs
- 1 teaspoon vanilla extract
- 1/2 cup buttermilk

For the Frosting:

- 1/2 cup unsalted butter, softened
- 2 cups powdered sugar
- 2 tablespoons Abuelita chocolate tablets, finely grated or melted
- 2-3 tablespoons milk or heavy cream
- 1 teaspoon vanilla extract

Instructions:

1. Preheat your oven to 350°F (175°C). Line a muffin tin with cupcake liners.

2. In a medium bowl, sift together the flour, cocoa powder, baking powder, baking soda, and salt. Stir in the finely chopped Abuelita chocolate tablets.

3. In a large mixing bowl, cream together the softened butter and granulated sugar until light and fluffy.

4. Add the eggs one at a time, beating well after each addition. Stir in the vanilla extract.

5. Gradually add the dry ingredients to the wet ingredients, alternating with the buttermilk, beginning and ending with the dry ingredients. Mix until just combined.

6. Divide the batter evenly among the prepared cupcake liners, filling each about 2/3 full.

7. Bake in the preheated oven for 18-20 minutes, or until a toothpick inserted into the center of a cupcake comes out clean.

8. Remove the cupcakes from the oven and let them cool in the muffin tin for a few minutes before transferring them to a wire rack to cool completely.

9. While the cupcakes are cooling, prepare the frosting. In a mixing bowl, beat the softened butter until smooth.

10. Gradually add the powdered sugar, beating until creamy and well combined.

11. Stir in the grated or melted Abuelita chocolate tablets, milk or heavy cream, and vanilla extract, mixing until smooth and fluffy. Adjust the consistency with more milk or powdered sugar if needed.

12. Once the cupcakes are completely cooled, frost them with the Abuelita chocolate frosting using a piping bag or spatula.

13. Garnish the cupcakes with additional grated Abuelita chocolate, if desired.

14. Serve and enjoy these delicious Chocolate Abuelita cupcakes as a delightful dessert or snack!

These Chocolate Abuelita cupcakes are a wonderful way to enjoy the rich and comforting flavors of Mexican chocolate in a classic dessert form. They're perfect for special occasions, gatherings, or simply as a sweet treat for yourself and your loved ones.

Mexican Brownies with Pecans

Ingredients:

- 1 cup (2 sticks) unsalted butter
- 2 cups granulated sugar
- 4 large eggs
- 1 teaspoon vanilla extract
- 1 cup all-purpose flour
- 3/4 cup unsweetened cocoa powder
- 1 teaspoon ground cinnamon
- 1/2 teaspoon chili powder (optional, for a spicy kick)
- 1/4 teaspoon salt
- 1 cup chopped pecans
- Powdered sugar, for dusting (optional)

Instructions:

Preheat your oven to 350°F (175°C). Grease a 9x13-inch baking pan or line it with parchment paper.
In a saucepan, melt the butter over low heat. Remove from heat and let it cool slightly.
In a large mixing bowl, whisk together the granulated sugar, eggs, and vanilla extract until well combined.
Gradually pour the melted butter into the egg mixture, whisking constantly until smooth.
In a separate bowl, sift together the flour, cocoa powder, ground cinnamon, chili powder (if using), and salt.
Gradually add the dry ingredients to the wet ingredients, stirring until just combined.
Fold in the chopped pecans until evenly distributed throughout the batter.
Pour the batter into the prepared baking pan and spread it out evenly.
Bake in the preheated oven for 25-30 minutes, or until a toothpick inserted into the center comes out with a few moist crumbs attached.
Remove the brownies from the oven and let them cool completely in the pan on a wire rack.
Once cooled, dust the top of the brownies with powdered sugar, if desired.
Cut the brownies into squares and serve.

These Mexican Brownies with Pecans are rich, fudgy, and infused with warm spices, making them a delightful twist on classic brownies. Enjoy them with a glass of milk or a scoop of vanilla ice cream for a delicious treat!

Mexican Orange Cake

Ingredients:

For the Cake:

- 2 cups all-purpose flour
- 1 1/2 teaspoons baking powder
- 1/2 teaspoon baking soda
- 1/4 teaspoon salt
- 1 cup granulated sugar
- 1/2 cup unsalted butter, softened
- 2 large eggs
- 1 cup fresh orange juice
- Zest of 1 orange

For the Orange Syrup:

- 1/2 cup fresh orange juice
- 1/4 cup granulated sugar

For the Orange Glaze:

- 1 cup powdered sugar
- 2-3 tablespoons fresh orange juice
- Zest of 1 orange (optional, for garnish)

Instructions:

Preheat your oven to 350°F (175°C). Grease and flour a 9-inch round cake pan or line it with parchment paper.
In a medium bowl, whisk together the flour, baking powder, baking soda, and salt until well combined. Set aside.
In a large mixing bowl, cream together the granulated sugar and softened butter until light and fluffy.
Beat in the eggs, one at a time, until well combined. Stir in the orange zest.
Gradually add the dry ingredients to the wet ingredients, alternating with the fresh orange juice, beginning and ending with the dry ingredients. Mix until just combined.
Pour the batter into the prepared cake pan and spread it out evenly.

Bake in the preheated oven for 25-30 minutes, or until a toothpick inserted into the center of the cake comes out clean.

While the cake is baking, prepare the orange syrup. In a small saucepan, combine the fresh orange juice and granulated sugar. Heat over medium heat, stirring occasionally, until the sugar is dissolved and the mixture is slightly thickened. Remove from heat and set aside.

Once the cake is done baking, remove it from the oven and let it cool in the pan for 10 minutes.

Use a toothpick or skewer to poke holes all over the top of the cake.

Pour the prepared orange syrup over the warm cake, allowing it to soak in.

Let the cake cool completely in the pan on a wire rack.

While the cake is cooling, prepare the orange glaze. In a small bowl, whisk together the powdered sugar and fresh orange juice until smooth.

Once the cake is completely cool, drizzle the orange glaze over the top. Garnish with orange zest, if desired.

Slice and serve the delicious Mexican Orange Cake.

This Mexican Orange Cake is moist, flavorful, and bursting with citrus goodness. It's perfect for any occasion and sure to be a hit with your family and friends!

Lime Margarita Bars

Ingredients:

For the Crust:

- 1 1/2 cups graham cracker crumbs
- 1/4 cup granulated sugar
- 1/2 cup unsalted butter, melted

For the Filling:

- 4 large eggs
- 1 1/4 cups granulated sugar
- 1/2 cup fresh lime juice
- Zest of 2 limes
- 1/4 cup all-purpose flour
- 2 tablespoons tequila (optional)
- 1 tablespoon triple sec or orange liqueur (optional)

For the Topping:

- Powdered sugar, for dusting
- Lime slices, for garnish (optional)

Instructions:

Preheat your oven to 350°F (175°C). Grease or line a 9x9-inch baking pan with parchment paper.
In a medium mixing bowl, combine the graham cracker crumbs, granulated sugar, and melted butter for the crust. Mix until well combined.
Press the crumb mixture evenly into the bottom of the prepared baking pan.
Bake the crust in the preheated oven for 8-10 minutes, or until lightly golden brown. Remove from the oven and let it cool slightly.
In another mixing bowl, whisk together the eggs and granulated sugar until well combined.

Stir in the fresh lime juice, lime zest, flour, tequila (if using), and triple sec or orange liqueur (if using) until smooth.

Pour the filling over the partially baked crust, spreading it out evenly.

Bake in the preheated oven for 25-30 minutes, or until the filling is set and the edges are lightly golden brown.

Remove the baking pan from the oven and let the bars cool completely at room temperature.

Once cooled, refrigerate the bars for at least 2 hours, or until chilled and firm.

Once chilled, dust the top of the bars with powdered sugar.

Cut the bars into squares and garnish with lime slices, if desired.

Serve and enjoy these refreshing Lime Margarita Bars!

These bars are a delightful combination of tangy lime flavor with a hint of tequila and triple sec, reminiscent of a classic margarita cocktail. They're perfect for parties, gatherings, or simply as a sweet treat for yourself and your loved ones. Cheers!

Chocolate Avocado Mousse

Ingredients:

- 2 ripe avocados
- 1/2 cup unsweetened cocoa powder
- 1/2 cup maple syrup or honey (adjust to taste)
- 1 teaspoon vanilla extract
- Pinch of salt
- Optional toppings: whipped cream, fresh berries, chopped nuts, shaved chocolate

Instructions:

Cut the avocados in half, remove the pits, and scoop the flesh into a blender or food processor.
Add the unsweetened cocoa powder, maple syrup or honey, vanilla extract, and a pinch of salt to the blender or food processor.
Blend or process the mixture until smooth and creamy, scraping down the sides as needed to ensure everything is well combined.
Taste the mousse and adjust the sweetness if needed by adding more maple syrup or honey.
Once the mousse reaches your desired sweetness and consistency, transfer it to serving bowls or glasses.
Cover the bowls or glasses with plastic wrap and refrigerate the mousse for at least 30 minutes to chill and firm up.
Before serving, garnish the chocolate avocado mousse with toppings of your choice, such as whipped cream, fresh berries, chopped nuts, or shaved chocolate.
Serve and enjoy the creamy and indulgent Chocolate Avocado Mousse!

This mousse is rich, creamy, and decadent, with the added benefit of being healthier than traditional mousse recipes thanks to the avocado. It's a perfect dessert for chocolate lovers and a great way to incorporate more nutrient-rich avocados into your diet.

Pumpkin Empanadas

Ingredients:

For the Dough:

- 3 cups all-purpose flour
- 1/2 teaspoon salt
- 1 cup unsalted butter, chilled and cut into cubes
- 1 large egg
- 1/4 cup cold water
- 2 tablespoons white vinegar

For the Filling:

- 1 cup canned pumpkin puree
- 1/4 cup brown sugar
- 1 teaspoon ground cinnamon
- 1/2 teaspoon ground ginger
- 1/4 teaspoon ground nutmeg
- 1/4 teaspoon ground cloves
- Pinch of salt

For Frying:

- Vegetable oil, for frying

For Dusting (Optional):

- Powdered sugar
- Ground cinnamon

Instructions:

In a large mixing bowl, whisk together the flour and salt. Add the chilled butter cubes and use a pastry cutter or fork to cut the butter into the flour until the mixture resembles coarse crumbs.
In a small bowl, beat the egg. Add the cold water and white vinegar to the beaten egg and mix well.

Gradually add the egg mixture to the flour mixture, stirring until the dough comes together. You may not need to use all of the egg mixture. The dough should be soft and slightly sticky.

Shape the dough into a ball, wrap it in plastic wrap, and refrigerate for at least 30 minutes.

While the dough is chilling, prepare the pumpkin filling. In a mixing bowl, combine the canned pumpkin puree, brown sugar, ground cinnamon, ground ginger, ground nutmeg, ground cloves, and a pinch of salt. Mix until well combined. Set aside.

Once the dough has chilled, preheat your oven to 350°F (175°C) and line a baking sheet with parchment paper.

On a lightly floured surface, roll out the chilled dough to about 1/8-inch thickness. Use a round cutter (about 4-5 inches in diameter) to cut out circles of dough.

Place a spoonful of the pumpkin filling onto one half of each dough circle, leaving a small border around the edge.

Fold the dough over the filling to create a half-moon shape. Press the edges firmly to seal, then crimp the edges with a fork to ensure they are tightly sealed.

Heat vegetable oil in a deep skillet or pot to 350°F (175°C).

Carefully place the empanadas in the hot oil, a few at a time, and fry until golden brown on both sides, about 2-3 minutes per side.

Remove the fried empanadas from the oil and drain them on paper towels to remove excess oil.

Transfer the drained empanadas to the prepared baking sheet and bake in the preheated oven for an additional 10-12 minutes to ensure the filling is heated through.

Once baked, remove the empanadas from the oven and let them cool slightly before serving.

Optionally, dust the warm empanadas with powdered sugar and ground cinnamon before serving.

Serve the delicious Pumpkin Empanadas warm or at room temperature. Enjoy!

These Pumpkin Empanadas are a delightful fall treat, with a deliciously spiced pumpkin filling encased in a flaky pastry crust. They're perfect for dessert, snacks, or even breakfast on chilly autumn days.

Mexican Chocolate Chip Cookies

Ingredients:

- 1 cup (2 sticks) unsalted butter, softened
- 1 cup granulated sugar
- 1 cup packed brown sugar
- 2 large eggs
- 1 teaspoon vanilla extract
- 2 1/4 cups all-purpose flour
- 1/2 cup unsweetened cocoa powder
- 1 teaspoon baking soda
- 1/2 teaspoon salt
- 1 teaspoon ground cinnamon
- 1/2 teaspoon cayenne pepper (optional, for a spicy kick)
- 1 1/2 cups semisweet chocolate chips
- 1/2 cup chopped Mexican chocolate (such as Ibarra or Abuelita)

Instructions:

Preheat your oven to 350°F (175°C). Line baking sheets with parchment paper or silicone baking mats.
In a large mixing bowl, cream together the softened butter, granulated sugar, and brown sugar until light and fluffy.
Beat in the eggs one at a time, then stir in the vanilla extract.
In a separate bowl, whisk together the flour, cocoa powder, baking soda, salt, ground cinnamon, and cayenne pepper (if using).
Gradually add the dry ingredients to the wet ingredients, mixing until just combined.
Stir in the semisweet chocolate chips and chopped Mexican chocolate until evenly distributed throughout the dough.
Drop rounded tablespoons of dough onto the prepared baking sheets, spacing them about 2 inches apart.
Bake in the preheated oven for 10-12 minutes, or until the edges are set and the tops are slightly cracked.
Remove the cookies from the oven and let them cool on the baking sheets for a few minutes before transferring them to wire racks to cool completely.
Once cooled, serve and enjoy these delicious Mexican Chocolate Chip Cookies!

These cookies are rich, chocolatey, and subtly spiced with cinnamon and cayenne pepper, making them a unique and flavorful twist on classic chocolate chip cookies. They're perfect for enjoying with a glass of milk or sharing with friends and family. Enjoy!